GYMNASTICS

PLAY·THE·GAME

GYMNASTICS

David Pearson

WARD LOCK

First published in Great Britain in 1991 by
Ward Lock Limited
Villiers House, 41–47 Strand
London WC2N 5JE
A Cassell Company

Text set in Helvetica
by Chapterhouse Ltd, The Cloisters, Formby, L37 3PX
Printed in England by Clays Ltd, St Ives plc

**British Library Cataloguing in Publication
Data**
O Pearson, David   ✓
    Gymnastics. – (Play the game)
    1. Gymnastics
    I. Title   II. Series
    796.44

    ISBN 0–7063–6972–6

ACKNOWLEDGEMENTS

The author and publishers would like to thank
Supersport for supplying the photographs
reproduced in this book.

**Natalia Lachenova, USSR. Extension
should be shown throughout the body
and here she shows that the body
extends through the fingers and the toes
expressing her total committment to the
floor exercise.**

CONTENTS

FOREWORD

David Pearson has a vast experience of performance coaching with all age ranges and coach education at all levels. His lifelong involvement in the sport of Gymnastics has been of great benefit to the governing body, not only in this country but in the other countries that he has visited and lectured.

In this book David provides all the answers to those newly motivated to enter the sport and gives a great deal of homework help to children outside Club time. It will be an ideal manual for anyone wishing to become involved, either as a Coach, Judge or a performer. Schoolteachers can gain great benefit from it and will be able to find the right pathway to enhance and develop their lessons.

I would regard it as an excellent background book to the many schemes which the governing body of British Gymnastics now run to encourage and support people who wish to purposefully participate in a sport which offers a lifelong involvement.

JOHN ATKINSON MBE FBISC
Technical Director BAGA
Chairman BISC

Terry Bartlett, GB, showing splits position on the Floor.

HISTORY &
DEVELOPMENT OF
GYMNASTICS

Wherever groups of people have settled they have found time to exercise, whether it be for recreation or for protection. The earliest civilization started approximately 6000 years ago in what is now called Iran and Iraq (Mesopotamia). There, the 'black-headed people', those who established the city-states, often warred with one another, living by the adage 'rule by strength'. The Egyptians, too, enjoyed respect for their knowledge of agriculture, building and mathematics as well as their armies. In the Indus Valley, a further river valley civilization shows signs of physical development through their elaborate ritual bathing pools.

It was not until the Greek civilization that a more defined and precise form of sport and exercise was seen. Exercise developed due to the needs of a constant rivalry between city-states. The exercises were performed for military ends, and it is here that the word 'Gymnastics' was first used. The boys and youths practised naked and so the Greek word *gumnos* (naked) formed the root for all aspects of this type of activity. The gymnasium was the sand-covered open area where the participants trained. The older youths were trained by the gymnastes, and

the exercises were called gymnastics.

Built around the gymnasium was the palaestra which was basically a number of rooms where lectures took place, and participants could change and relax. This was strictly a man's world, comparable to a British Gentleman's Club. It is interesting to note that the European word gymnasium still means a place of academic learning (especially one which has an accent on the classics), whereas in Britain the same word really refers to the palaestra itself.

Greece suffered the same fate as other great civilizations. Although the seeds of democracy and culture can be seen in its writings it was nevertheless a society based on slavery and colonization. Greed, jealousy and rivalry intermingled to cause its downfall. Indeed, it is recorded that the Olympic Games, first seen in 776BC were soon banned due to too much commercialism and horiffic acts of cruelty.

With the downfall of the Greek and later Roman Civilizations, Europe fell into the Dark Ages. Very little was seen of gymnastics throughout this period except in the form of juggling and acrobatics performed by wandering bands of entertainers at fairs, markets and courts of the nobility.

It was not until the Renaissance that an attempt was made to use gymnastics. JCF Guts Muths working in Germany studied the Greek use of exercises and used them to formulate a basis of physical education. He used apparatus to develop the muscles of the body and tried to classify the exercises by anatomical means. His work was continued during the early part of the nineteenth century by a German, JF Jahn, and a Swede, PH Ling who developed a definite break in the concepts of gymnastics. Jahn developed the sport of gymnastics (German gymnastics) while Ling developed a system of gymnastics (Swedish gymnastics). The rivalry between these two forms of gymnastics is still inherent in British gymnastics.

Jahn used apparatus to develop certain physical and social attributes into the gymnasts. The vaulting horse, parallel bars and rings were used to strengthen the upper body; jumping a bar (like a high jump) strengthened the legs. His ideas were also very patriotic for he aimed at improving the physical aptitude of his compatriots.

Ling, however, based his work more on anatomical/medical lines and classified the exercises accordingly. He worked with and without apparatus regarding the movement of the body to be of prime importance rather than the acquisition of a skill. His work was accepted in many countries through his connections with the Association of Swedish Doctors.

The two forms, then, are very different:

Jahn's was a sport, while Ling's was a system of movement education. Jahn's German gymnastics started to develop in Britain but its progress was severely hampered. The climate did nothing to help (the first gymnasia were outside), and there was a severe lack of equipment. Later, the Great War took its toll of members of clubs, as did the 'German' image. Instead, England adopted Swedish Gymnastics as the basis of physical education in its schools. Clubs closed, equipment was thrown away and colleges of education frowned upon gymnastics as a sport. Added to this was the work carried out by R Laban who further studied Ling's work to devise a system whereby he proposed that a child could be physically educated through specific movements. The factors essential to all movements he defined as time, weight, space and flow. Many colleges of education combined this with the fundamentals of Ling's work to develop the bases of physical education. Unfortunately, German gymnastics suffered once again as it was derided because of its use of the word gymnastics and its limitations of purpose. Gymnastics as a sport suffered because of this and its popularity declined steadily through the 1950s and 1960s.

So, British gymnastics needed some enthusiasm injected into it. It was given this by the televising of Olga Korbut's 1972 Olympic routines. The tremendous impact that this Russian made on the general public allowed for wider coverage, transforming the interest in gymnastics beyond all previous recognition. The British Amateur Gymnastics Association (BAGA), in partnership with the Sunday Times, devised Award Schemes that schools soon used within their physical education lessons. The tremendous interest that these produced meant that clubs were created in and outside of schools. Such enthusiasm was further boosted by the Romanian star Nadia Comaneci who electrified world audiences with her perfect 10s. The BAGA capitalized on this and gymnastics flourished throughout the country. The forms of gymnastics that the BAGA now caters for has increased too, and courses for coaches, competitions, exhibitions, advice and information became available from the BAGA headquarters. The BAGA now serves its members in the following forms of gymnastics:

Artistic gymnastics Men's and Women's Competitive

Rhythmic gymnastics Competitive and Recreational

Sports acrobatics Men's and Women's Competitive

General gymnastics Pre-school, Special Needs, Recreational, Adults and Displays

Artistic gymnastics

Artistic gymnastics is often referred to as Olympic gymnastics and is directly related to Jahn's German gymnastics. It is competitive and is governed by the International Federation of Gymnastics (FIG). There is a section for males and females. The males work on six pieces of apparatus: floor, pommelled horse, rings, vault, parallel bars and horizontal bar. The females work on four pieces of apparatus: vault, asymmetric bars, beam and floor.

Rhythmic gymnastics

Rhythmic gymnastics is a sport specifically for females. It is dance orientated and requires the gymnast to work with small hand apparatus such as the ball, rope, hoop, ribbon and clubs. Many rhythmic gymnasts work a free exercise and often work in pairs and trios as well as groups.

Sports acrobatics

Sports acrobatics is performed in single and mixed sex groups in various numbers where balances are to the fore. Gymnastic skills and some dance are also required. One section of the sport is known as tumbling where skills are shown on a specially sprung trackway.

General gymnastics

General gymnastics are non-competitive. This form of gymnastics encompasses the whole range of age groups under the umbrella of what could be termed gymnastics for leisure. Through this section, the BAGA caters for the pre-school child with their parent(s), the non-competitive gymnast of all ages and special needs gymnasts (especially those suffering from Down's Syndrome). The accent is on participation and it is fast becoming the largest section of the BAGA, through the use of Award, Reward and Participation Schemes.

It is in the area of general gymnastics that a fundamental change in the provision of gymnastics by the BAGA has taken place. One can see a move away from Jahn's narrow concept of gymnastics as a sport and general gymnastics provides an avenue whereby gymnastics can be utilized by all people, of all ages and abilities, to explore physical movement for their own enjoyment and aspiration. While Korbut and Comaneci kindled the public's awareness of the sport of gymnastics, their level was such that few could aspire to. But gymnastics is about exercise and exercise should be available to all. With the development of general gymnastics may come the acceptance of both Ling's and Jahn's ideas. Both had useful and worthwhile objectives: unfortunately both were subject to inflexibility and narrowness of thought. With the more diverse opportunities being offered by general gymnastics hopefully there will now be a fusing of the two forms, giving a balance to and a fuller understanding of, 'gymnastics'. In this way gymnastics can be elevated and recognized as a physical art form capable of use by all.

EQUIPMENT & TERMINOLOGY

Before looking at the skills and fundamentals of the sport of gymnastics we should first familiarize ourselves with the equipment the gymnast uses. This is best done by dividing the pieces of apparatus into two – those used by the men and those used by the women in artistic gymnastics. In addition, the training aids most used to develop skills and the personal equipment that the gymnast should have are covered in this chapter.

MEN'S ARTISTIC GYMNASTIC APPARATUS

Floor area

This is a 12 m² of matting which is carpet covered. The floor is sprung to aid the gymnast in their skills. It has a sloping surround of approximately 1 m which acts as a safety margin. The floor square is a very expensive item and most clubs cannot afford this. Instead, squares are often made up of mats and sometimes clubs use just one line of mats on which to practise the major skills and tumble runs.

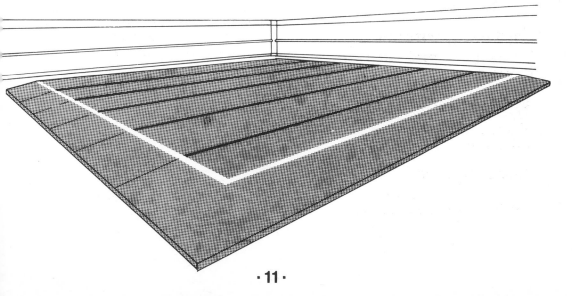

Pommelled horse

Originally, a pommel horse body had four legs and a tail. Today, many horses have only two legs, the tail has disappeared and two handles have been added. The handles, generally made of wood, and the top of the horse, covered by leather, must be used in a routine.

Rings

The rings were once divided into the swinging rings and still rings. The type that has been retained is the still rings. Rings can be suspended from a ceiling beam or from a frame. A frame is preferable as it imparts a flex which the gymnast can use to advantage and gives a better awareness to the gymnast.

Vault

Used by both males and females, the vault is the quickest performed. Males work the vault in a lengthwise direction while females use it crosswise. A spring board is used to assist the gymnast onto the horse. Many clubs use the pommel horse as a vault by simply removing the handles but now that spring-assisted vaults are manufactured this is not advisable.

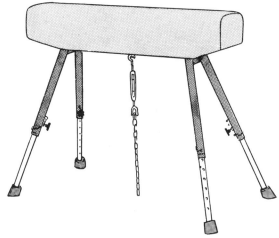

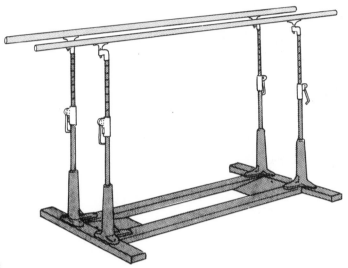

Parallel bars

The parallel bars have altered significantly in their manufacture. At one time they were extremely stiff but they now have a flex in them. Fibreglass bars are available nowadays but these haven't been accepted yet by the FIG. To ensure safety if the bars were to break there is a metal inlay set longitudinally through the bars.

Horizontal bar

The horizontal bar is made of high tensile steel which is extremely flexible. As with the rings, the bar can be fixed by chains forming a frame. In many clubs, bars can have wall-supported bars to save on space.

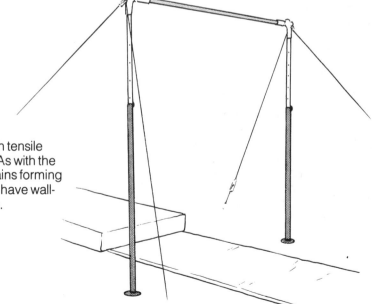

Lacraniola Filip, Romania, showing total body control and extreme amplitude on the beam.

WOMEN'S ARTISTIC GYMNASTIC APPARATUS

Vault

This apparatus is the same as for men except that it is worked crosswise. Women in most competitions are allowed two attempts at the vault while the men are only allowed one.

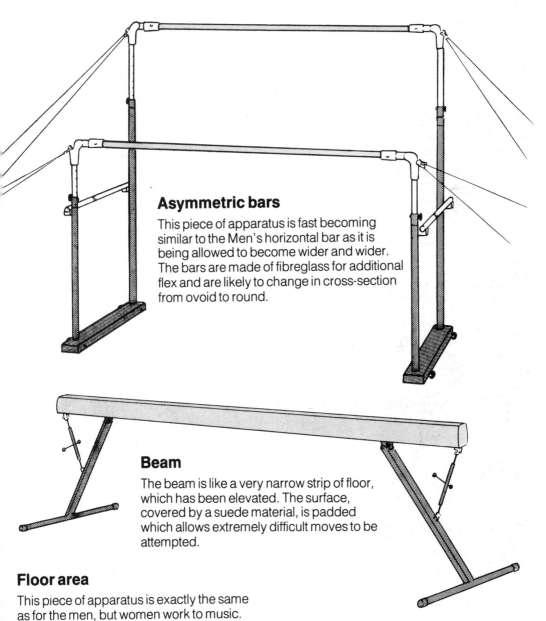

Asymmetric bars

This piece of apparatus is fast becoming similar to the Men's horizontal bar as it is being allowed to become wider and wider. The bars are made of fibreglass for additional flex and are likely to change in cross-section from ovoid to round.

Beam

The beam is like a very narrow strip of floor, which has been elevated. The surface, covered by a suede material, is padded which allows extremely difficult moves to be attempted.

Floor area

This piece of apparatus is exactly the same as for the men, but women work to music.

TRAINING AIDS

There are many training aids in use, some are commercially manufactured, many are made by coaches and/or parents. Often a coach will make up temporary equipment utilizing whatever is available at the time. The following shows some of those aids that are in common use in many clubs around the country.

Safety Pits

Either sunk into the ground or built like a giant box, safety pits are filled with soft, crushable cubes of foam. They safely arrest the gymnast and are used mainly under the swinging pieces of apparatus such as the rings, asymmetric bars and horizontal bar. But they can also be used in many situations where a difficult move is being practised or learnt. They are responsible for a huge progress being made in complex skill acquisition.

Trampolines/Trampettes

These are used by gymnasts to enable them to learn moves requiring spatial awareness. The trampoline provides elastic energy to the gymnast allowing him/her to concentrate on certain aspects of the skill. Trampolines and trampettes are dangerous pieces of equipment and should only be used under the supervision of a qualified coach.

Safety belt

This is a belt that is attached to the gymnast's waist by a system of ropes and pulleys. A coach can hold a gymnast free of the ground using this device and help him/her to practise a move safely.

Safety mats

These have the same function as a safety pit, providing a safe landing area if a gymnast makes an error. Landings should be made on feet, backside, or back and there should be a non-slip mat beneath the crash mats as an additional precaution.

Benches

A very useful but often neglected piece of equipment, the bench can be used for many, many activities. It can become a beam; a slope for rolling or stepping down; a strength training aid; a platform for dismounting from. It can provide height from which to better practise a move, and with the addition of another bench can be a makeshift set of parallel bars.

Mushroom

Used for training for the pommel horse, this piece of equipment is best described as an upsidedown saucer on legs. The same effect can be gained by putting two springboards together with the open ends touching each other.

Trolley Trainer

Used with a bench, a trolley trainer can help the gymnast to strengthen the upper body, especially in certain moves for horizontal bar, asymmetric and parallel bars and rings. By pulling him/herself up the trolley using the rope and pulleys, the gymnast slowly builds up strength by moving the trolley into an increasingly steep slope.

Boxes

It is often necessary for the coach to stand above the apparatus or the gymnast, and boxes can provide a study platform for this. They can also be used by the gymnast to practise certain moves, act as supports when strengthening and stretching or as a basic piece of apparatus for vaulting. Many boxes are made of wood but soft foam is being used to good effect nowadays.

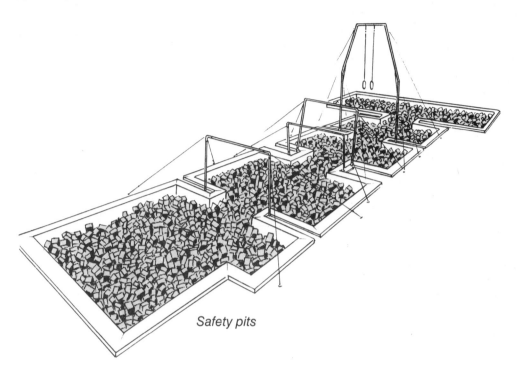

Safety pits

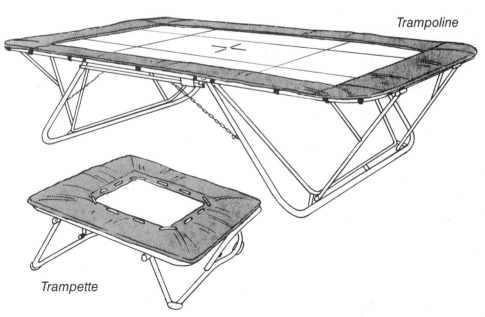

Trampoline

Trampette

GYMNASTICS

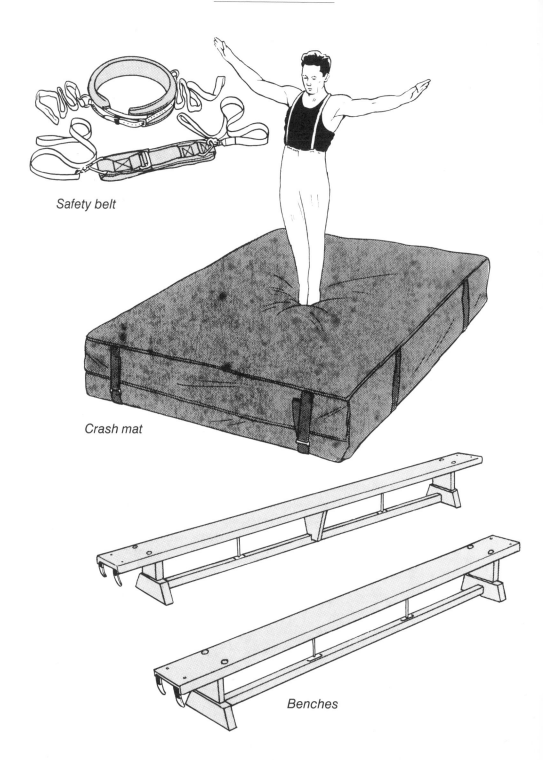

Safety belt

Crash mat

Benches

Mushroom

Boxes

PERSONAL EQUIPMENT

Clothing

Leotard   Leotards are made of two-way stretch material that hugs the body. The one-piece designs ensures that they will not fall off during competition and training.

Shoes   Some gymnasts like to wear shoes for the floor area, vault or beam. They should have a non-slip sole and be a snug fit. They should follow the line of the feet and look smart in wear otherwise one can easily lose points for poor form. Many gymnasts prefer to wear non-slip socks only, especially on the swinging forms of apparatus.

Trousers   Men are obliged to wear trousers on some of the apparatus at a certain age. As with the leotard, they should stretch and fit tightly around the waist. The traditional white or cream colour is advantageous as the chalk marks do not show.

Hair clips   Women need to ensure that their hair is neat and tidy. If the hair is long then a simple pony tail held with an elastic band at the nape of the neck is sufficient. If the hair is shorter then more clips may be necessary.

Handguards   These are the most essential piece of equipment. As gymnasts increase their skills and work on the more difficult and complex skills their hands become hot and sore; handguards can provide some protection against this soreness. At the same time, the highly complex skills require much greater grip of the bar and handguards are made with this in mind. When gymnasts reach this level of work they will have learnt what types of handguard are best. A few years ago most coaches had to make their gymnasts' handguards for them but nowadays there are a number of manufacturers making them. A beginner does not really need to work with handguards unless they are in their teens or above.

First aid

The gymnast should be ready for sore hands and possible rips of the skin, they are a part of the sport. The hands take a severe strain and should be looked after which means that after training they should be cleaned and then soaked in hot water. Any rough skin should be scraped off using a pumice stone, file or similar abrasive tool. The hands should be lightly smeared with a hand cream. If skin has ripped, the loose skin should be cut off and then the above treatment followed applying a medicated cream over the wound.

Elastic tape and an elastic bandage are further useful items to have in the first aid kit. Tape can often be used to prevent soreness or to use as an emergency handguard. Elastic bandage is often used to stop the handguards slipping up onto the wrist where they rub and chaff the skin. They can also be used for support if a strain occurs.

Training aids

Many gymnasts find it useful to have the following items with them:

Notebook and pencil: for jotting down points, new moves, etc.

Music tapes: of floor routines (best to have a copy).

Elastic strands: made either from elastic rope obtainable from yachting chandleries, or pieces of bicycle tyre inner-tubes. These can be used for stretching, warming up and practising certain movements.

Code of Points: often there are occasions where a gymnast wants to check the difficulty of a move, or a rule. The *Code of Points* should be regarded as the gymnast's Bible.

Ian Shelley, GB, showing excellent concentration and good form.

GYMNASTICS TERMINOLOGY

The following words and/or phrases are those that you may come across when talking to other gymnasts, coaches or judges.

A-bars   These are asymmetric bars which the girls use. They are sometimes referred to as High and Low Bars.

Angle   When a coach refers to this he is generally talking about the angle that is made between the hip and the leg and the angle between the arm and shoulder. The term is often qualified by saying opened or closed which means it is either a straight or piked position.

Ariel   This means a move that is done without any support on the ground such as a somersault-type move. Sometimes the term 'free' is also used.

Average   A master judge will find the two middle scores from a group of judges and will add these together. The total will then be divided by two to find the average. Usually this is the mark that the gymnast will then receive.

Basics   The fundamental skills of the sport. Certain moves can be seen on each piece of apparatus and must continuously be practised. The handstand is one such basic move.

Blocks   Small pieces of wood or rubber that are attached to handguards to help the gymnast keep a good grip on the apparatus. They are usually used on the horizontal bar, asymmetric bars and rings.

Catch   Often used with the phrase 'release and catch' which refers to moves which leave the apparatus and then regrasp it within the routine. Moves such as Delchevs, Gaylords, Geingers and Tkatchevs, all release and catch and are named after the person who first showed it in competition.

Circles   Can mean two different things. It can be the circle described when a gymnast swings completely round the horizontal bar, asymmetric bars, or the rings. It can also be when a gymnast describes a circle with both legs horizontally on the floor or the pommel horse. (These circles can also be shown on other pieces of equipment but are not as popular.)

Combinations   Each piece of apparatus have certain rules that must be adhered to which give the character of that piece of apparatus, these are referred to as combinations.

Cone of swing   Is generally used to describe the pendulum swing that is apparent when someone swings on the rings.

Dish   A certain shape of the body that is used extensively in gymnastics. It gives an aesthetic line to the body and is also a mechanically strong body position. If you were to lie on your back on the ground and lift your shoulders and legs each about 15 cms off the ground this would give you the approximate shape. The arms should be above the body in line with it or the hands resting, palm down, on the top of the thighs.

Dismount   Is the term used to describe the last move of a routine.

Double   This can mean two things. One of the meanings is the same as horizontal swinging of the legs as described under *Circles*. The other is used as an abbreviation for double somersault.

Elements   Another word for a move or skill.

Elephant   A certain type of strength move into handstand that is used a great deal. It is performed in the same way that you often see elephants performing handstands in the circus. Often a gymnast will say its just like lifting the weight of an elephant!

Execution   How a move is performed, either with good or bad style.

Flairs   A certain way of performing double leg circles (see *Double* and *Circles*) where the legs are split. It was first performed by an American called Thomas and thus are sometimes referred also as Thomas flairs.

Flighted   A move done which shows a bounce out of the floor, normally off the hands. It can also refer to a release and catch move where the body actually is flighted before it catches again (see *Catch*).

Full-in   This is an abbreviation for a full twist in a somersault. It is generally used with double somersaults. A full-in back out for example would mean that a gymnast performs a full twist in the first somersault and then another somersault before landing. (This is often used as a dismount or as a move in its own right on the floor.)

Giants   A move where the gymnast swings completely around the apparatus through the vertical plane. (Also known as a longswing or a grand.)

Grand   See *Giants*.

Hold   A move which must remain still for two seconds.

Inlocate   A circular movement about the shoulders, used mainly on the rings.

Jury   A panel of judges. However, it is also thought of as a higher group who check the scores being given by the judges. A jury is often formed with the president of the judging panel and the superior judge of each piece of apparatus. The score can be altered by this body if they feel it is warranted.

Kip   See *Upstart*.

Line   Is often used to describe the shape that the gymnast shows. The gymnast should strive to show straight positions wherever possible. It can also refer to the line which forms the perimeter of the floor area. The line width itself (usually 50 mm) is part of the floor area – if a gymnast steps on it they will still be in, if they step over it they will be deducted accordingly.

Linkage   A way in which elements are joined together.

Longswing   See *Giants*.

Loops   A training aid for learning *Giants*. The loops are made of two lengths of very strong webbing that are attached to the bar and the wrists of the gymnast. They allow the gymnast to stay on the bar while practising. Loops can also refer to double leg circles which are done at the end of the pommel horse.

Mount   The first move that starts a routine.

Move   An element or skill.

Originality   New or unusual moves or linkages of movements. A judge can award a bonus factor for originality.

Overall   The final score when the compulsory (or routine set) and the voluntary routine marks are added together (see pages 26–9 for a more detailed breakdown).

GYMNASTICS

Ping Term used when a gymnast comes off the horizontal bar, parallel bars and rings, asymmetric bars, without meaning to! This normally happens as a result of an incorrect body shape that makes the bar, or rings whip at the wrong time resulting in the gymnast being catapulted off. It is very dangerous and re-emphasizes the need for correct body shaping exercises as a basis of all work in the gym.

Planche A held position in support or suspension which requires strength to maintain it. Is seen most often on the rings.

Puck A body position half way between a pike and a tuck shape which is often used while training certain moves.

Range of movement The limits of movement about the various joints of the body. These limits are determined by the structure of the joint, the muscle surrounding it and the connective tissues within.

Release Same meaning as for *Catch*, but more precisely means the letting go part.

Rotate The act of turning about one of the three axes of the body such as when performing a somersault, cartwheel and full-turn jump.

Scale A balance or hold part.

Series Used mainly in ladies' gymnastics where it describes three or more single elements that are linked together forming a continuous movement.

Support A position where you are normally in balance on the apparatus.

Tariff The value that a vault is given. Every vault is given a difficulty rating of A, B, C or D, and each of these are given a value. In men's gymnastics, the A is worth an 8.7 tariff. In women's, A vaults are tariffed up to 9.00.

Tkatchev A release and catch move that is used widely by both men and women on the horizontal bar and asymmetric bars (see *Catch*).

Tumble A number of elements that are linked together in a continuous movement. Normally these are done on the floor and consist of acrobatic elements, so are different to a series which can be gymnastic in nature. (Gymnastic can mean moves that are leaps, turns, body waves, etc rather than acrobatic which is recognized as a somersault- or handspring-type movement.)

Underswing A swinging move that is performed below the apparatus, most frequently seen on the parallel bars.

Upstart A particular way of getting into support on a piece of apparatus. (Also known as *Kip*.)

Violation A violation occurs whenever something is done that is not in character with the type of apparatus work described under combination requirements.

Virtuosity Is shown when the best possible performance is shown. It is a special quality of movement which people would applaud because of its artistry.

Whites Another name for trousers worn by male gymnasts.

Wrap A movement often executed on the asymmetric bars where the hips flex about the lower bar. Not so much in vogue today as the bars have been widened so much that it is not possible to perform it. Also used to describe what happens when a gymnast's handguards get stuck on the bar, normally because they are too long. A very dangerous situation as it can damage the wrist.

THE BASIC RULES

Competitive gymnastics at international level is governed by the International Federation of Gymnastics (FIG) who publish a *Code of Points* that all coaches and gymnasts must follow. It is upgraded every four years immediately after the Olympic Games. Competitive gymnasts have to compete in two ways:

Compulsory (or Set) Routines
Voluntary Routines

COMPULSORY ROUTINES

These, as the name suggests, are routines performed on each piece of equipment which are laid down by the governing body. All gymnasts entering World and Olympic Championships must do these same routines and they are judged as to how well they perform them.

The compulsories specify exactly which moves, linkages and patterns should be performed. The governing body decides how many marks they will award for each part of the routine and also what will be deducted for performing any part incorrectly. There is a very small allowance for bonuses to be given, but these are for virtuosity only.

VOLUNTARY ROUTINES

These types of routines, done on each piece of equipment, have to follow certain rules that offer a framework. Each gymnast can interpret and personalize the routines as long as they keep within the rules as set down in the *Code of Points*.

As there are only basic rules to abide by, the gymnast and coach must be sure they fully understand their sport.

JUDGING THE VOLUNTARY ROUTINES

In very general terms male and female gymnasts follow the same basic rules. Obviously there are slight differences but the following will give an overall view or understanding of both. The rules are divided into four components: difficulty; execution; combination, and bonus. When scoring the routines, the judges have to take each of these components into consideration.

Difficulty

Each move performed by a gymnast is categorized by the FIG into degrees of difficulty. There are four degrees, A, B, C, and D where A is the easiest and D is the hardest. Each of these degrees, or values, is given so many tenths of a point. The A value has a value of two-tenths (0.2), B has a value of 0.4, C has 0.6, and D has 0.8.

Depending on the type and level of competition, a gymnast has to show a minimum number of moves that have certain levels of difficulty. If a gymnast does not do the number set then each one missing will be deducted from the total number of points offered for this component. However, if the gymnast does *more* than required he/she will *not get more marks*. This is a very important point that must be understood from the outset. The total value that can be achieved for difficulty is laid down in the rules; for men it is 4.0 points, and for ladies it is 3.0 points. To illustrate this further, look at the following example using the Men's Code:

Difficulty: 4.0 points.
This is made up from the following values:

6 × A value	(6 × 0.2 = 1.2)	
4 × B value	(4 × 0.4 = 1.6)	
2 × C value	(2 × 0.6 = 1.2)	
0 × D value	(0 × 0.8 = 0.0)	
	Total:	4.0 points

Gymnast 1: does not put enough moves in:

3 × A moves	(3 missing = deduction of 0.6)
3 × B moves	(1 missing = deduction of 0.4)
1 × C move	(1 missing = deduction of 0.6)

Total deductions for difficulty = 1.6 points
Thus: Difficulty = 4.0 − 1.6 = 2.4 points

Gymnast 2: puts all the moves in that are required:

This gymnast will have no deductions as he has shown all the moves required. Therefore his score will remain at 4.0 points for difficulty.

Gymnast 3: puts in more than is required:

e.g. 10 × As, 6 × Bs, 9 × Cs and 2 × Ds

This gymnast will receive just 4.0 points for difficulty. He will not gain any more marks for doing all these extra.

This is an important point as it can be seen that the gymnast who puts in more will gain nothing from it. All too often he becomes tired by so much effort and looses marks through bad form. A good coach will only put in the minimum number of moves necessary, with beginners they will often put in less. It is far better to look elegant, neat and in control than to be all bent arms and out of puff at the end of a routine. The main objective of gymnastics is to be artistic.

Execution

Gymnasts should always be aware of how they look while performing their routines. They should try to be neat and tidy, to show they are in control and show the movements in good style. This is the first tenet of gymnastics and it is for this reason that more marks can be lost under this component. Men can lose up to 4.4 points, while women can lose up to 5.1 points. A judge will look at two main things under execution:

1. Form of the body.
2. Technique of the skill.

Under form of the body, the judge can deduct marks for bent legs, bent arms, separation of legs and hollow positions where not required. Under technique, the judge will look at the position of the gymnast and compare it to the ideal which is mechanically effective for performing that particular skill (for example, executing a handspring with the shoulders forwards of the hands would be unsound).

Both form and technique errors are divided into deviation from the ideal and have a sliding scale of deductions:

	Men's deductions	Women's deductions
Small errors	0.1	0.05–0.20
Medium errors	0.2–0.3	0.25–0.40
Large errors	0.4–0.5	0.45–0.50

Combination

Each piece of apparatus has certain fundamental requirements which must be shown in addition to the difficulties. This ensures that the routine is constructed with basic building blocks that give it a character which is acceptable for the piece of apparatus being worked on. The following example shows the floor area combination requirements for both men and women. It indicates how they will perform differing routines:

Men's floor area combination requirements:
1. Must work for 50–70 seconds.
2. Must have three tumble runs, one of which must contain a C-value difficulty.
3. Must have a hold part which is held on one arm or leg for two seconds.

4. Must have a B-value difficulty which consists of strength.
5. Should show harmony between the differing types of movements.
6. Should use all the floor area.

Ladies' floor area combination requirements:
1. Must work for 70–90 seconds.
2. Must have three tumble runs, one of which must contain two somersaults or one which has a D-value difficulty.
3. Should have a gymnastic series of moves which contains three elements.
4. Should have one gymnastic element that has a B-value difficulty.
5. Should have a connection of a gymnastic and acrobatic move.
6. To end the routine with a B-value difficulty.
7. To interpret the music used harmoniously with the body movements.
8. To show changes in speed and levels within the routine.

In the same way as described for difficulty, the judge can deduct marks for missing out any of these requirements. Again, however, there is a maximum amount of deductions permissable. In men's work it is 1.0 point, while in women's it is 1.5 points.

Bonus

Judges can also award a small number of points under the bonus component. Men can be given up to 0.6 points and women up to 0.4 points.

Men can be given marks for showing very difficult moves in their routines (all D-valued moves are classed as RISK as are some combinations of C-valued moves which are known as 'upgraded D-values'). Men can also gain marks for showing new or rare movements (classed as originality), and for executing a move with panache (classed as virtuosity). Women can be given bonus points for any additional natural D-value parts included in their routine and for demonstrating originality.

The scoring system

By combining the total marks available for the difficulty, execution and combination components, each gymnast starts with a number of marks; this is known as the base mark. In order to achieve the perfect 10.00, the gymnast must not lose any marks from the base mark and, in addition, gain points from the bonus component for doing excellent work. So, for men, the base mark is 9.40 comprising:

Difficulty   = 4.00
Execution   = 4.40
Combination = 1.00
               9.40

To the base mark a judge can add 0.60 bonus marks to make a possible total score of 10.00.

Thus the gymnast can score a 10.00 if all the required moves are worked, there are no deductions for executions, all the necessary combinations are put into the routine and the judge is shown certain movements that warrant bonus for risk, originality and virtuosity. It is extremely difficult to get the perfect 10.00 and requires years of training; but it is possible.

For women, the base mark of 9.60 is made up of:

Difficulty   = 3.00
Execution   = 5.10
Combination = 1.50
               9.60

With a bonus of 0.40 points, the total possible score arrives at 10.00 points.

JUDGING THE COMPULSORIES

The compulsories are determined by the FIG and have different values for moves and linkages. The difficulty, combination, risk and originality are within the routine already. For the compulsories, the judge starts with a base mark of 9.80 and is allowed to award just 0.20 points for virtuosity for the men. The women's base mark is set at 10.00 points.

WATERING DOWN THE ROUTINES

As beginners cannot do routines that contain all the necessary skills, the British Amateur Gymnastics Association (BAGA) has devized Codes to enable different standards of gymnasts to compete. The Men's Voluntary Code is called the *Junior Code* and is divided into two parts known as the A and B Codes. The A Code is the harder of the two. The women have devized the *Novice* and the *Intermediate Codes*. All these Codes are used at club, county, regional and national level competitions, up to the 16+ age level.

In the same way, the World and Olympic compulsories are too difficult for beginners and so the BAGA has a graduated scheme which leads up to them. These are known as the National Development Sets (NDPs) and are used for both girls and boys. The NDPs and FIG Codes are all available from the BAGA.

Li ping Huang, China, on parallel bars showing perfect body line.

RULES CLINIC

What happens if a gymnast steps out of the area during a routine?

The line of the floor area is in, thus if the gymnast steps on the line no points are deducted. But if the gymnast steps outside of the line, for no matter how many steps, 0.1 point is deducted. Every time a gymnast goes out of the area, this deduction of 0.1 point is made.

What happens when a gymnast falls?

There is a specific deduction for a fall which is 0.5 point.

What happens if a piece of equipment breaks during a routine?

In both mens and womens gymnastics the discretion is with the judges or sometimes the organiser of the competition, in consultation with the chief judge. The gymnast would be allowed to continue the routine without loss of points.

What would happen if a gymnast wore the wrong clothes?

There would be a deduction of 0.30 point for men and 0.10 point for women as it is considered to be unsportsmanlike behaviour. Correct dress for men is long, solid-coloured trousers and footwear on pommels, rings, parallel bars and the horizontal bar. Shorts, with or without footwear, or trousers with footwear are permissible on both the vault and floor. Women must wear a sport leotard which must be in good taste and they are allowed to choose whether or not to wear footwear on each piece of apparatus.

What happens if a gymnast goes overtime?

The end of a routine on floor and beam (the only ones that have time limitations) is signified by a bell or whistle. If a man then continues, the moves outside of the end whistle are not considered and points are deducted on a sliding scale dependent on the length of time over. On the beam, 0.20 points are deducted.

What would happen if someone stopped me during my routine or vault?

The judge would use his/her discretion and probably allow you to retake the attempt.

If, during a routine, a gymnast changed his/her routine what would the judge do?

The judge can only judge what he/she sees. The judge does not know the routine and will not know it has been changed. So, as long as the harmony and flow is not broken, the routine will stand as it is performed. Obviously, if the compulsory routine is changed then there will be definite deductions which are covered in the *Code of Points*.

What happens if the music goes wrong during a gymnast's routine?

The gymnast should continue to perform his/her routine. It is probable that the judge will allow a second attempt if it is found there was a fault with the equipment after consultation with the organizers.

What is the best thing to do if a gymnast continuously falls off during a beam routine?

On the beam the gymnast is allowed to fall off as many times as she likes. However, each time she falls, a deduction is made of 0.50 point and the gymnast is given 10 seconds to remount. This time is separate from the time for the routine itself. If the gymnast does not remount within 10 seconds, the routine is deemed finished.

Is it better for a coach to support a gymnast to achieve a move in a routine?

Any assistance given by a coach to a gymnast is met with the deduction of 0.50 point. Sometimes a coach is quite happy to forfeit this because he/she may want to develop a particular move in competition or know that the routine will flow better with a little help. Be careful of assistance in the compulsories, however, as it can make the routine void in some cases.

If a gymnast gets confused during a competition and does his/her compulsory instead of his/her voluntary, what deductions would occur?

The judge would be forced to award a zero mark.

If a gymnast stops him/herself from falling off a piece of apparatus by hanging onto a post would this be the same as a fall?

This is a little subjective. The judge would have to assess whether or not the gymnast definitely fell or whether he/she stopped and would deduct marks accordingly. For women, this would most likely mean a deduction of 0.30 point, while for men it could be in the range of 0.20–0.50 point.

How long should a balance be held for?

To be designated as a hold, a balance should last two seconds. It is important that holds are separated from other balances because gymnasts are penalized on some apparatus (especially on the beam and the parallels) for holding more than a prescribed number of balances.

If a gymnast runs into the vault can he/she vault again?

If the gymnast were male, he would get a zero mark and he could not make a second attempt as in most competitions men are only allowed one vault (the only competition where two vaults are allowed is in the finals of the Olympic and World Championships). For women it is a little more complicated for they are generally allowed two vaults. If a female gymnast were to touch the horse, this attempt would get a zero mark but she would be allowed an attempt at her second vault. However, if she had not touched the springboard or the horse, the vault would not be invalid. In this case she could try again up to a maximum of three more times. If the maximum number of times is used then the last time will automatically incur a 0.50 point penalty. In the compulsories she would be allowed only two more attempts.

How do the judges arrive at the final score?

The top and bottom judges' scores are disregarded and the remaining scores are averaged. This average is then checked with limits that are set in the *Code of Points* as the eventual score must fall within the limits set if it is to be accepted by the master judge. The master judge, however, can also alter the score if it does not fall in line with his or hers.

Why is it normally very quiet during a gymnast's routine?

This is because a gymnast usually needs to concentrate and other gymnasts respect this. Also, deductions can be made if a gymnast is spoken to by his/her team mates.

What does a green light, or flag, signify?

This means that the gymnast should start his/her routine. Conversely, a red light or flag instructs the gymnast not to start the routine.

TECHNIQUE

When starting out as a gymnast a beginner must be aware that the body should first be physically prepared to enable him to achieve certain techniques. This is the fundamental part of a gymnast's work. One could compare it to a carpenter who first has to learn how to use chisels, saws and measurements to achieve quality work. In the same way, a seamstress must first learn how to use needle and thread before she can make a mannequin's dress. So it is with the gymnast.

BODY PREPARATION

The gymnast must have basic body abilities that can be used to develop quality of physical movement. Thus the gymnast should know what body preparation is and it should become an integral part of each gymnastic session. Below is shown how this body preparation can be developed into a programme of work:

1. Objectives
2. Warm-up
3. Flexibility
4. Strength
5. Tone
6. Skills
7. Analysis

Objectives

When a gymnast goes into a gym or starts a session at home, he/she should know what he/she is doing and why. A coach will plan short, medium and long term goals for their gymnasts taking into account their ages, standards and competitions. A gymnast can, however, help him/herself at home. If he/she knows that he/she is weak in certain areas of the work, he/she can devize practices and exercises at home that will improve them. Developing the habit of exercising at home will not only improve the gymnastic standard but it will also help keep the body and mind healthy.

Warm-up

The human body must be attuned to the forthcoming work both mentally and physically. The warm-up should be planned to ensure that all of the body is functioning and areas that are going to be used more should be emphasized. Basically, if the body is to work it will need energy and this comes from oxygen. So the warm-up must provide the means whereby increased lungfuls of air are taken in. As muscles also work better in a warm environment a gymnast should make sure he/she works in a space where there is a comfortable temperature. Good, warm, comfortable clothing is a must.

The warm-up is normally divided into activities which work:

1. Large muscle groups through game-type activities.
2. Large muscle groups, but more specifically, working systematically up or down the body.
3. Specific muscle groups by relating the activities to the work that is going to be done during the session.
4. Specific muscle groups to work on the area the gymnast has a deficiency in.

GYMNASTICS

Flexibility

This is sometimes referred to as the range of movement. It is defined as the ability of the joints of the body to move to the maximum extent allowed by the structure of that joint and its connective muscle and tissue. Flexibility should be worked on within the session once the body has been thoroughly warmed-up and this can be at any time within the session. Some gymnastic coaches work on flexibility immediately after the warm-up but this is not necessary. It is probably better to do it during the session itself or even at the end when the body is at its warmest (or should be!). By putting the flexibility at the end of the session the body can then warm-down gradually which is as important as the warm-up.

To plan the flexibility exercises, the body can be divided into three major ranges of mobility and three minor ones. The major ranges are the shoulders, spine and hips; the minor ranges are the elbows and knees, wrists and ankles, and fingers and toes. Each of these joints works in certain directions and has specific limitations and the type of movements possible can be seen by looking at the various joints. For example, the shoulders and hips are ball-and-socket joints; the elbows are hinge joints; fingers are saddle joints, and the toes are plane joints.

When working on flexibility it is worthwhile knowing which exercises are best used to improve the range of movement of each joint. Basically there are two ways to improve flexibility when training:

1. Ballistic stretching, where the arm or leg is rhythmically swung to its furthest outward position. This form of stretching is not used very much in gymnastics as it does not really stretch the muscles fully. It can also cause muscle tears if done too vigorously. However, it is good for warming-up.

2. Static stretching, where the joint is slowly extended to its outermost position. This is the method mainly used by gymnastic coaches as it is the most effective form of stretching. It can be worked in three ways:

   a. Active stretching: where the gymnast himself extends the joint over a period of about 10–30 seconds.

   b. Passive stretching: where an external force is applied to the gymnast's joint, normally by the coach for a period of approximately 6–30 seconds.

   c. PNF stretching: where the gymnast works first passively or actively, then tries to work the joint in the opposite direction to its stretch for about 10 seconds. After this, the joint is relaxed and passive or active stretching is resumed.

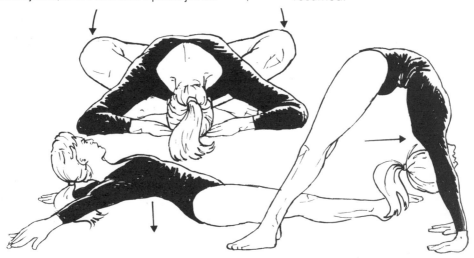

Some active, passive and PNF stretching techniques used to improve flexibility.

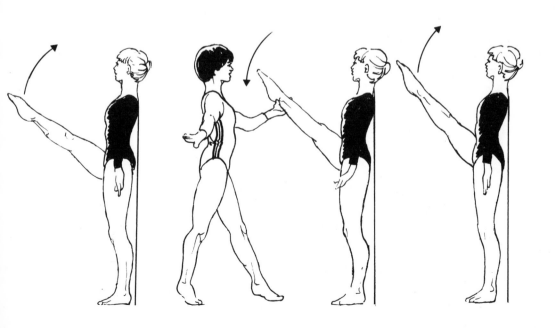

Strength

An often misused word, strength can mean many things and it is important to be aware of the differences.

Muscular strength is the ability of a muscle to overcome a force. The larger the muscle the greater the force it will overcome. In order to improve the amount of force needed to be overcome it is necessary to train with near maximum forces (the number of times this can be done is small as the muscle quickly tires).

Muscular power is the speed at which a muscle can overcome a force. It is a very important part of gymnastics training because the movements that are used are quick and explosive. It is therefore necessary to train for this type of strength with fairly heavy forces that can be moved rapidly about 8–10 times.

Muscular endurance is best enhanced by performing an exercise many times (over a long period of time) applying only a light force. It is very important to work on muscle endurance as a gymnast needs to perform a movement or skill many times to learn and improve it.

Tone

Muscles need toning as well as strengthening as the body needs to be fixed in particular shapes and positions and muscles are placed under strain to do this. To improve the tone of any muscle, the demands made upon it must be increased. In addition, the shape of the body is equally important, so exercises should be developed to match the shapes and skills required. This is known as the specificity of training. It is therefore important to provide a programme of work that exercises the muscles to develop their various functions, and it should be closely related to the skills that are hoping to be achieved.

An example showing muscle-toning specifity within training. Here the gymnast does many press-ups but it does not improve his/her ability to hold a handstand. It would be better to do the second exercise as it more closely resembles the position needed.

Skills

The various skills that a gymnast needs to acquire will be based on the type of gymnastics he is involved in. Men performing artistic gymnastics have to work on six pieces of apparatus while women work on four; a rhythmic gymnast uses hand apparatus, and a sports acrobat works a lot of balance positions. A list of all the moves possible in gymnastics would soon be in the thousands, but they can be grouped together – known as structure groups – and the FIG shows each group and the moves within them in the *Code of Points*.

Each structure group has basic skills which are taught to beginners and from them other skills can be developed and increased in complexity and difficulty. The skills shown in this chapter (see pages 40–78) form the basic techniques that a beginner would need. They are first analyzed in their ideal form and then exercises are given which could be practised at home to help the gymnast to gain mastery of them using very simple or no equipment.

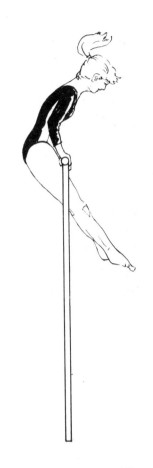

Analysis

When working on a programme of work you should be able to tell if it is working, is effective and suitable. Every so often you should look at the programme and assess it in some way. It may be that the strength you are needing for a skill has been achieved, the flexibility required has not materialized, etc. The exercises have to be changed to ensure progress and often a different exercise will be more effective than another for a particular gymnast. Also changes can ensure interest is maintained which is an important factor to consider. Continually test yourself, keep a record of your progress, draw graphs and have a check-off list of skills. Try to devize a system that works for you. The best comment I ever heard was from a top Romanian coach who said, 'It doesn't matter how good a coach technically you are if the system you work in doesn't suit you, you will not succeed to your potential.' This can also apply to the gymnast.

So now you have the theory of gymnastics it is time to look at the skills to enable you to put it into practice. Each skill is shown in its ideal form and practice and conditioning exercises are also provided that can be worked on at home to help you to achieve the ideal.

NOTE: No matter how simple each part skill looks, by working slowly on them you will be putting in good habits for the future. Practice all these parts separately, do not think they are too easy for it is in developing these fundamentals well that you will gain quality of work.

Tong Fei, China, exemplifies the explosive power needed in modern mens vaulting.

A forward roll.

SKILLS FOR HOME PRACTICE

Forward rolls

The legs should be straight at (1) with the head well tucked in at (2). The legs should be kept as straight as possible for as long as possible before being tucked in to help you to stand (3). The hands and arms should reach forward without touching the ground to stand (4).

Practice exercises

1. To help feel the straight leg action, rest the soles of your feet against a wall or chair and straighten your legs. To enable you to do this, your hands must be placed a good distance from the feet.
2. Practise the late tucking-in position from a shoulder balance as in positions (2) to (3) and at the same time work on reaching forward to stand up.
3. Try to set up some form of slope that you can roll down so that all the parts can be practised more easily.

Conditioning exercises

1. Hold the press-up position for 8 seconds but with your feet raised from the ground.
2. Practise press-ups.
3. Practise fast sit-ups drawing up your knees to meet your chest.

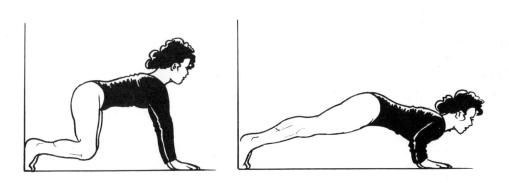

Practice exercise 1. Lines drawn on the floor add incentive for stretching further and further away from your feet.

Backward rolls

The body should fold at (1) with the hands moving back having the fingers pointing in the same direction as the toes (2). The legs should be straight throughout. The hands touch the floor *before* the backside at (3) to gently place the body on the floor. The hands *very quickly* move backwards to be placed by the ears with palms down on the floor (4). As the hips start to move over the head and hands the gymnast pushes down into the floor so that the hips are lifted (5) so enabling the head to move through (6). Many finishing positions are possible, but it is best to learn the straddle as it helps in the actual rolling action (7).

Practice exercises

1. Feel the folding position (1) by working against a wall.
2. Practise the move into position (4) by putting the hands flat on the floor by the ears.
3. Improve this movement by moving the hands from the sides of the body, as in position (3), to the ears, as in position (4).
4. Practise sitting down without actually rolling over, *i.e.* moving from positions (1) to (4).
5. If possible, practise the complete move down a slope, or ask one of your parents to lift you at the hips to help you feel your head moving through as in positions (5) and (6).
6. Practise the whole movement on a flat surface finishing with a straddle.

A backward roll.

Conditioning exercises

1. Practise half press-ups (*i.e.* from your knees, not your feet) and then clap your hands together to make you push harder.
2. Lie on your back with your head by a wall and knees bent. Push away from the wall to feel the push needed for this skill.
3. Standing upright, cross one leg over the other. Try to keep both legs straight as you fold down as far as possible. Hold this position for about 8 seconds at first building up to 30 seconds. Repeat with the other leg crossed over.
4. Repeat exercise 3 but this time sitting on the floor with your feet raised. It might be easier to practise this one first without crossing your legs.

Practice exercise 1. A wall offers excellent support when practising the fold-over.

Half-turn jumps

The head and neck should remain relaxed and fix visually on a point until the last possible moment (1). To get a good spring, bend the legs slightly as at (2). The arms move into the body to aid the spin (your hands can move up over your head as illustrated; they can fold onto your chest, or ycu can do a mixture) (3). As the body completes the turn, the head moves round quickly to fix on another point which is 180 degrees from the original one (4). The arms are taken out sideways to slow down the rotation and the legs bend into a demi-plié position to finish.

Practice exersises

1. Mark a square on the floor to act as a guide to the half-turn. Start facing one side of the square, and finish facing the opposite side.
2. Work on your arm movement in co-ordination with your legs. The arms circle down as the legs bend, they then cross over in front of your body. As they continue to be lifted up so the legs straighten. After a few repeats of this action, do the same again, but jump as your arms move up.

3. Look at an object, move your feet to twist round to face the opposite direction while continuing to keep the object in view. Once your body has made the half-turn, move your head round to look at an object which is 180 degrees from the first.
4. Do the same practice as exercise (3) but with the correct arm action as in exercise (1). Then finally do it with a jump and turn.

Conditioning exercises

1. It is important to keep the back straight in this skill, and the exercises here help to develop this aspect.
2. Leg strength must also be worked to give jumping power. Remember that if you want power, then fast movements should be done with fairly heavy loads. The body itself can be used as the load. To achieve greater leg strength, stand on the edge of a step and lift yourself up onto the ball of the feet (ankle elevations); or jump with both feet together over a number of objects (squat jumps).
3. Mark a height on a wall and then jump up and touch the wall beyond it. Keep increasing the height as you improve.

Conditioning exercises 1, to strengthen the back muscles.

A half-turn jump.

Full-turn jumps

Because the body turns through 360 degrees, the arms have to be kept into the body longer than for the half-turn jump. Therefore, the same principles apply as for the half-turn, but taking this into consideration. If you now concentrate on the head position you will notice that you have to move the head position from the starting point to it again at the end of the move. The important point is to keep the head fixed on the original point for as long as possible before moving it – this is the most important part of the skill. Use the same practice and conditioning exercises as those suggested for the half-turn jump.

A full-turn jump.

Hayley Price, GB, showing good line in a longarm with full-twist vault.

Gymnastics

Handstands

The step-in should be a good stretched position with the arms held well forward and to the sides of the ears (1). The fingers reach forwards to the floor first so that the balance can be taken up by 'gripping the floor' (2). The body line should be straight and vertical (3), for most gymnasts this will mean that their head is held naturally between the arms (some very supple gymnasts can keep the straight line with the head held out). The position out of the handstand should be shown with the arms held as before, but with the first leg coming down close to the hands to enable the body to be lifted up easily (4).

Practice exercises 2, 3 and 4.

A handstand.

Practice exercises

1. Practise reaching well forwards on the floor keeping one leg straight behind you as in position (2).
2. Kick up from your bed against the wall.
3. Walk up backwards against a wall.
4. Kick against a wall into a handstand.

Conditioning exercises

Flexibility at the shoulders needs to be worked at. A bed or wall are good supports, and circling scarves or ropes add strength to the upper arms and shoulders. Always aim to keep your back straight.

Conditioning exercises for handstands.

Pirouettes

The handstand should be thoroughly mastered first (1). To enable the handstand to move the body should go slightly out of balance (2). It is then possible to move one hand a quarter turn (3). The weight will be transferred to this support arm and the other hand should be lifted to move it a quarter turn so producing a half-turn while in the handstand (4). This movement is executed slightly differently if working on the parallel bars. The half-turn is started before the vertical is achieved. However, at this stage it is best to just work on the basic position.

Practice exercises

1. Draw a square on the floor with sides about shoulder width apart. Use the corners to place the hands in the quarter-turn positions.

2. Stand with your side to a wall. Kick up to handstand then do a quarter-turn so that your back is against the wall. When you can do this create the second quarter-turn to step out of the handstand to the side of the wall facing the opposite direction from where you started.

3. Ask one of your parents to help you with this exercise. Do a handstand on his/her feet and then, while holding your hips, he/she should step back a quarter-turn with one foot. By stepping forwards a quarter-turn with the opposite foot, a complete half turn is made.

Conditioning exercises

The same exercises used for the handstand will suffice.

A pirouette.

An arabesque.

Arabesques

The support foot should be turned out slightly to ensure that the hips are kept square (1). The support leg is kept slightly bent while the back leg is raised (2). The knee and the foot of the back leg should be kept facing the floor to ensure that the hip is not twisted. As the back leg reaches the maximum height the support leg straightens and the upper body starts to move down (3). The arms are kept slightly a shoulder width apart pointing either forward or back. The body assumes a horizontal position so that the back knee and the shoulder form a straight line (4). Some gymnasts show a higher lift on the back leg to gain virtuosity.

Practice exercises

1. Draw a line on the floor and stand with your foot to each side of it. Decide which is to be your support leg.
2. Practise stepping to the side of the line with your support leg so that the foot is turned out slightly. Find the most comfortable position and concentrate on the squareness of the hips.
3. Face a wall standing slightly less than an arm's stretch away from it. Using the wall as support with one of your hands, place the support foot correctly and start to raise your back leg – you will feel your hips twist out slightly. Correct the squareness by keeping the knee and foot facing down.

4. Do the arabesque away from the wall. As the support leg straightens when the back leg raises to its maximum height, you will feel a pinch in the back. It is at this point that the upper body should be slowly lowered to the horizontal. Practise finding this pinch point so that the movement can be co-ordinated.

Conditioning exercises

1. Practise keeping your feet wide, balletic foot positions are excellent for this. The five positions are shown here.
2. Practise the back leg position using a support to lean on, but remember to always keep your back straight.
3. Good flexibility is needed at the hip joint. PNF stretching is the best form of exercise, but active exercises are almost as good.

The five positions of the feet as used by dancers.

Conditioning exercises 3.

Half-levers

This is an important skill in gymnastics for both boys and girls and should be worked continuously. For a straddled half-lever, the torso should be slightly leant back and the head held upright and not pushed forwards onto the chest. The fingers should point very slightly outwards and should be slightly bridged to aid in gripping the floor. The legs should be straight with the feet pointed being held slightly higher than the hips.

A half-lever.

Practice exercises

1. Use a chair that has arms to it, two chairs close to one another, or piles of books or boxes to support you. Push up so that you are supported by the arms off the floor. Do this exercise first with the legs bent then try keeping them straight in front of you at right angles to the body (in a piked position).
2. Practise supporting yourself by the hands with the knees resting on the elbows. This position is known as a Chinese balance. First hold the Chinese balance and then see if you can take the foreleg forward.

Practice exercise 2.

Conditioning exercises

1. Sit-ups.
2. V-holds (hold each one for 10 seconds).
3. V-sits (15 times)

Conditioning exercises 1, 2 and 3

Straddle stand lift to handstand

This move is often referred to as 'the elephant lift' and it is an important skill in gymnastics as it is used on many pieces of apparatus. It builds up strength and is a balance and strength move in its own right. Used in conjunction with the half-lever, the elephant upgrades the difficulty of the skill. The hips are drawn up above the hands so that they are very slightly forwards of them and at the same time the legs are drawn in towards the

hands so that they are approximately 30 cms to each side of the hands (1). The legs are lifted from the floor until they reach the vertical position bringing them in line with the body (2). The legs are then brought together so that a handstand is held (3).

A straddle stand lift to handstand.

Practice exercises

1. Doing a piked headstand, moving into a full headstand, allow yourself to lean slightly into a wall. This exercise will help you to gain the correct hip and shoulder position. Repeat, but as a handstand.
2. Practise handstands in the same way but without the aid of a wall and starting with your feet resting on a raised block.
3. Move from a piked into a full handstand with your hands resting on a raised block. It will be much harder raising your legs to a full handstand in this position. Much harder than (2).

Conditioning exercises

The exercises illustrated here aid flexibility and strength.

Conditioning exercises for the 'elephant'.

Cartwheels

The handstand position is fundamental to the cartwheel and it is essential that the handstand is thoroughly understood before going onto the cartwheel. Always think of the cartwheel as a handstand with a quarter turn and the basic skill will then be learnt correctly.

The cartwheel has exactly the same approach as the handstand (1), but as the hands are about to touch the floor they are turned through 90 degrees (2). The leading leg is brought down close to the far hand to allow the upper body to be lifted up. The second, or trailing, leg should be held up momentarily.

There are three basic finish positions: the gymnast can face sideways, inwards or outwards depending on the next move that is to be performed. All these finishes should be experienced.

Practice and conditioning exercises

See those used for the handstand on pages 48–9.

A cartwheel.

Vitali Scherbo, USSR, demonstrating virtuosity of technique on the pommel horse.

Round-offs

The round-off, sometimes called an Arab spring, is in the same family as the cartwheel as it has a similar pattern of movement. Again it is based on the handstand, but with the round-off, the hands are placed on the floor in the pattern shown here to help effect the half-turn. To enable the body to have more lift, so allowing it to half-turn, the chest is brought down forcefully towards the forward leg. The back leg rapidly kicks up (1) and (2). At the same time the arms slightly bend when they contact the ground so that as the legs swing through the vertical they are straightened against the floor. This action provides the lift to the movement. The body dishes as it passes the vertical which helps the upper body to rise; this is known as snapping-up (3). The round-off, as with the cartwheel, is a linkage movement leading into other moves such as the flic-flac and somersault. For this reason there are differing finish positions which need to be learnt with it. You will often hear a coach talk of a 'donkey-kick' action; this is the action that is used to practise this aspect of the skill.

The position of the feet and hands during a round-off.

A round-off.

Practice exercises

1. Work the handstand practices as shown on pages 48–9.
2. Practise down a step and use chalk on your hands to check where they are being placed.
3. Practise the donkey-kick action by executing steps (2) and (3) off a raised block.

Conditioning exercises

V-sits (see page 52), and dish shapes on your front and back (see page 56), are all valuable conditioning exercises for the round-off.

The finish positions for a round-off before leading into a flic-flac or a backward somersault.

Practice exercises 2 and 3.

The backward walkovers

The body is fully extended and straight to begin with with the front foot pointed (1). The shoulders are then extended backwards and upwards (2) while the hips move slightly forwards (3). As the backward movement is generated the head should be looking for the floor (4), and the forward leg should be lifted towards the splits position. As the hands touch the floor so the legs are further split by the first leg extending towards the floor behind (5). The support leg pushes up and the body now passes through the vertical with the body shape being kept straight (6). The first leg continues to be extended towards the ground through the split and comes to the ground fairly close to the hands to enable the upper body to be lifted (7). The second leg is brought to a horizontal position which is held momentarily before bringing the leg to the floor.

A backward walkover.

GYMNASTICS

Practice exercises

1. Stand fully stretched against a wall and lift the leg which will lead backwards.
2. Practise moving into the bridge position. Then do the same but lift one leg.
3. Kick out from a bridge position.
4. Walk up a wall and kick over.
5. Bend backwards to touch a wall and then bend back further, walking down the wall to reach a bridge position.

Practice exercise 2.

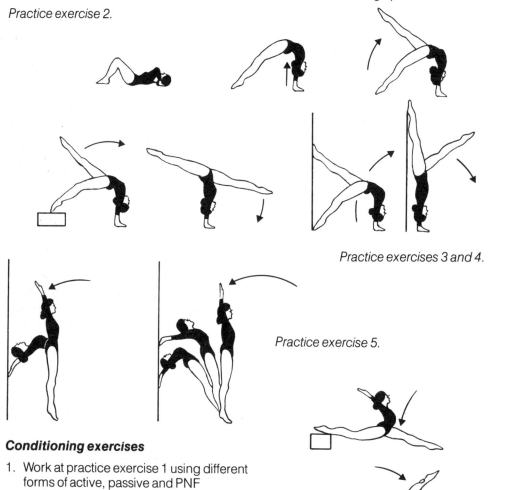

Practice exercises 3 and 4.

Practice exercise 5.

Conditioning exercises

1. Work at practice exercise 1 using different forms of active, passive and PNF stretching.
2. Practise the splits.
3. Practise the bridge as illustrated in practice exercise 2.
4. Move into a handstand with your legs doing the splits; hollow your back and straighten it again.
5. Work at the shoulder flexibility exercises given for the handstands on pages 48–9.

Conditioning exercise 2.

Monica Covacci, Canada, demonstrates why the straddle lift position is such an important basic movement skill, here seen in her Asymmetric Bars routine.

SKILLS FOR CLUB PRACTICE

The next skills should be done at the gym club with the guidance of a coach. However, the practice and conditioning exercises shown can be done at home and will help you to succeed in the skills when you are taught them. These skills are all moves that introduce flight into your repertoire and are the cornerstone movements for gymnastics.

The kip action

This action will give you the feeling associated with many movements that require a rapid opening of the hip angle. The action requires that the hips are slightly forwards of the hands and head (1). As the legs lift, so opening the angle at the hips, the hands start to push down (2). The legs continue to extend, opening the hip angle further while the arms push to straighten them so that the body moves through a path similar to a parabola (3).

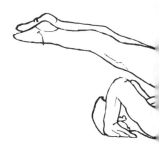

Practice exercises

1. Practise doing a headstand by walking in with the feet towards the head and hands until the feet can be lifted easily off the floor. When this has been mastered, do the same again with straight legs.
2. Do the headstand against a wall allowing the hips to fall slightly forwards.
3. Do a forward roll and reach into a straight leg headstand.
4. Do a shoulder balance, lower the legs backwards and then extend back up to the shoulder balance. Then move into a bridge position.

Conditioning exercises

1. From a bent leg handstand, kick to into a straight leg handstand against a wall. To increase the load, move from a straight leg headstand up into a handstand.
2. Practise bunny hops.
3. Lie on your back close to a wall with your head touching it and then push yourself away from the wall.
4. Practise V-sits as shown on page 52.
5. Practise piked to straight headstands.

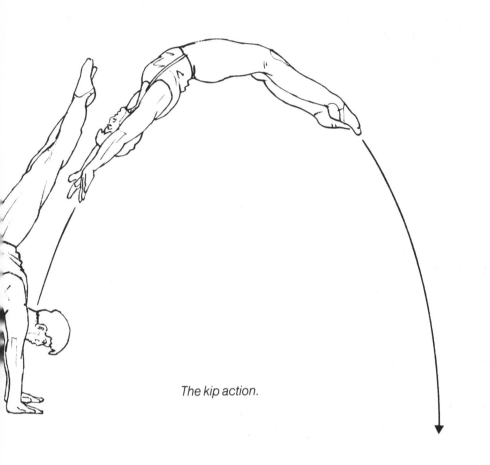

The kip action.

Conditioning exercise 2.

Handsprings

The first priority is for the gymnast to be able to hold an excellent handstand. The body is kept straight and moves well forwards with the arms kept in a straight line to the sides of the ears (1). As the hands touch the floor, the arms bend slightly and at the same time the back leg kicks rapidly over the hands aided by the straightening of the forward leg (2). The legs pass the vertical and join up just before the landing takes place (3). The body is kept as straight as possible throughout.

Practice exercises 3, 4 and 5.

A handspring.

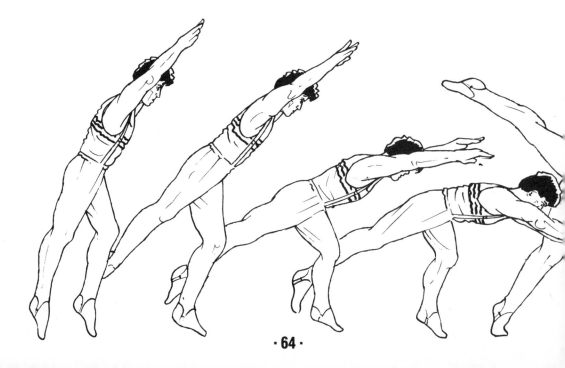

Practice exercises

1. Practise good stretches into a handstand position (see pages 48–9). Keep the shoulders slightly back from the hands. Rest your chest down on the thigh of the forward leg.
2. Kick to a handstand close to a wall, allow your legs to fall back against it and hold the position.
3. Practise the hurdle step as illustrated here.
4. Practise double bouncing. Always keep your body straight, reach into the floor and feel the bounce as you move up.
5. Blocking practice. By stopping the feet rapidly before they touch the floor you will experience the lift that occurs at the shoulders. This is what happens as the legs are brought together in the handspring.

Conditioning exercises

1. Stand close to a wall and bounce off it using your arms as springs.
2. Practise head- to handstand pushes as shown in conditioning exercise 1 for the kip action on page 63.
3. Practise extended squat jumps.
4. Swing your rear leg upwards using a wall for support as your torso moves forward.
5. Practise dorsal lifts.
6. Practise walking into a bridge down a wall as shown in practice exercise 5 on page 60.

Conditioning exercises 3 and 5.

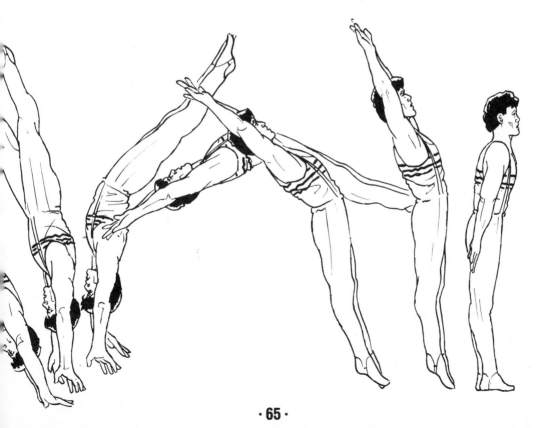

Flic-flacs

The flic-flac is acknowledged as the cornerstone of all gymnastic work. It requires courage as well as sound technique. Correct part-learning skill-work will pay off handsomely. The flic should fall backwards slightly with the back kept straight (1). The arms begin to swing to the front as the legs bend (2). The knees should be kept behind the feet at all times to ensure the movement continues to move backwards. The arms are swung forwards and backwards to pass the ears (ensure that the back does not hollow at this stage) (3). The legs start to straighten and the feet push into the ground at an angle to create a parabolic curve which is fairly low and flat (4). As the hands touch the floor the body should dish (5). The arms bend very slightly to aid in the thrust from the floor. The body will rotate so that the feet will move towards the floor while the hands lift up (6). It is important here that the body starts to rise up rather than the legs being allowed to go down. This is the same snapping-up action which was seen when dealing with the cartwheel (page 55) and the round-off (pages 56–7).

A flic-flac.

Practice exercises

1. Feel the position of the backward fall by leaning against a wall.
2. Fall back against a wall, using your hands to stop yourself hitting the wall too hard.
3. Sit down into an armchair or chair without using your arms.
4. Fall backwards onto your bed sending your arms above your head to stretch the body.
5. Practise the snapping-up action by using the donkey-kick practise illustrated on pages 56–7.

Conditioning exercises

1. Use a rope or scarf to increase mobility about the shoulders as described on page 49.
2. Rapidly raise your arms up and past your shoulders without creating a hollow in your back.
3. Move into a bridge position rapidly.
4. Lie flat on your back, knees bent and feet resting against a wall; then push yourself away from the wall along the floor.

DIFFERENT APPARATUS TECHNIQUES

For this type of work you will need to belong to a club and much of the work practised will be under the guidance of a coach. However, you can improve your skills by working at home on exercises that will condition you for the various moves you will learn in the club.

Useful training aids can be made up simply to help in many of the actions you will find described here. Ask your parents if they can make them up for you. Ask them to check that they are safe to use, and that they are stable and strong enough for your use.

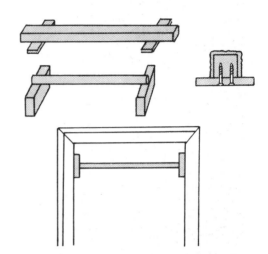

A beam can be made from a piece of 4 × 4 ins wood covered by carpet that is glued and/or stapled to the underneath; mini-bars can be used to practise bar and parallel bar skills, and a door bar fixed into a door frame can be used to practise swing actions. Ensure you have some form of padding under this bar.

Support position

The front support is a basic position on the bar and should be understood and practised correctly as it will help to develop moves with strength, style and efficiency. The hands should be in overgrasp with the arms straight. The shoulders should be slightly forward of the bar and the middle/upper part of the thigh should rest on the bar. The shoulders should be pressed down so that there is no sag across them.

Practice exercise

Sag at the shoulders and then push down. This can be done using two chairs as shown on page 52.

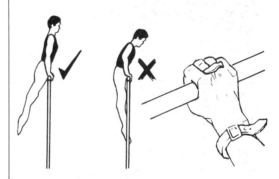

The correct support position is shown alongside an example of an incorrect support position together with a detail of the handgrip.

Mario Reichert, DDR, showing excellent form on the horizontal bar.

Upward circles

The legs are lifted towards the bar while the shoulders are 'dropped down' (1). The bar is kept at the hips as the rotation occurs (2). A fast wrist shift occurs to enable the arms to be in a support position (3). By stopping the feet momentarily the shoulders will lift, aiding them in their upward movement. The head is kept in line with the body at all times.

Practice exercises

1. Imagine kicking backwards over the bar.
2. If possible, walk up a slope.

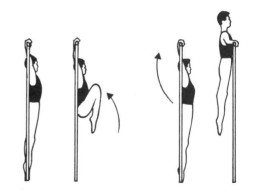

Practice exercises 1 and 2.

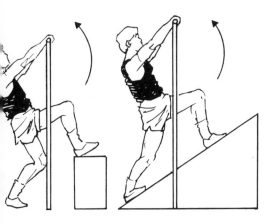

Conditioning exercises

1. Chin pull ups.
2. Knee pull ups.
3. Practise slow sit-ups first bending your knees to meet your chest, and then as V-sits (see page 52).

Conditioning exercises 1 and 2.

An upward circle.

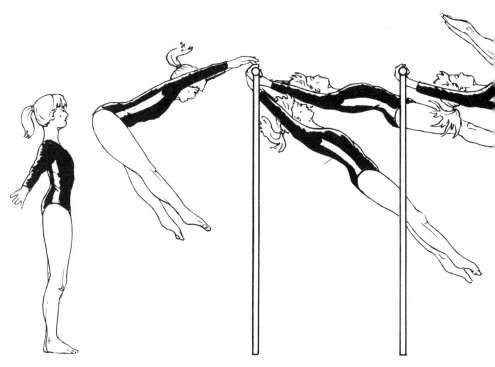

An upstart.

Upstarts

Read over the work for Kip Action on pages 62–3 first. There are many varieties of upstart possible. The basic movements are the same, however, and these are the opening and closing of the shoulder and hip angles. The upstart starts with a swing in overgrasp and rises at the front to about a horizontal position (1). The feet are brought to the bar by closing the hip angle rapidly (2). The legs are then slid upwards along the bar by closing the angle at the shoulders (3). As the bar reaches the hips, the arms bend slightly and the wrist shifts on top of the bar to allow the body to get into a support position (4). The feet are momentarily stopped to put the shoulders slightly in front of the bar (5). This helps the gymnast bear away from the bar in preparation for another move out of the upstart. It is best to continue the upstart in this fashion otherwise there will always be a hesitation at this point in your routine which can cost you marks.

Practice exercises

1. Practise swinging forwards beneath the bar to get the feel on step (1).
2. Practise moving forwards into the swing from a raised position to get the feel of the rising opening swing.
3. Practise step (2) by lifting your legs from a raised position while holding onto the bar.
4. Raise yourself into position (4) from the ground.

Conditioning exercises

1. Go into a headstand and lower and raise your feet with straight legs.
2. Hanging from the bar, lift your feet in front of you with straight legs.
3. Practise V-sits (see page 52).
4. Buy some elastic rope from a Yacht Chandlery, attach one end to a wall several feet up. Sit with your back to the wall, raise your hands in the air and bring them forward and down to the sides of your thighs, keeping your arms straight as you go.
5. Press down on a chair trying to close the angle at the shoulder and hold for 10 seconds (an isometric contraction).

Swings

As ladies' asymmetric bars are widening it is possible to teach the same swinging action for both girls and boys. It is important to learn the basic swing early on as it forms the basis for the longswing (sometimes called the giant or the grand).

In the basic swing the body should be straight and stretched on the downswing (1). As the body approaches the vertical position the hips should be slightly forward of the feet keeping the body still in a tight, stretched line (2). As the body passes through the vertical under the bar the hips should relax slightly and the feet are 'tapped' through to create a dish shape as the body swings forwards and upwards (3). As the body returns through its swing at the back, like a pendulum, remember to shift the wrist around the bar to ensure adequate grip.

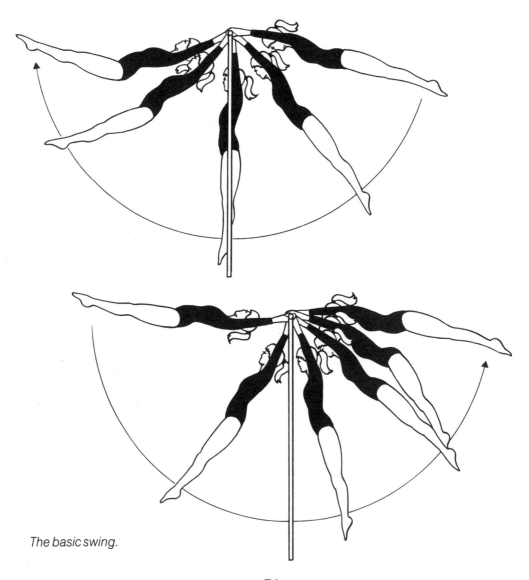

The basic swing.

Note: these diagrams are for information only and must not be attempted at home.

A back longswing and
a forward longswing.

Practice exercises

1. Swing beneath the bar. By changing your body shape as illustrated, you can feel your hip arching at the vertical.
2. Widen the swing slightly but do not go too high at the front. Remember to regrasp at the point A with the wrist; this is the point where there is danger of you being pulled off the bar.
3. Move from a handstand from a raised object at the foot of your bed onto your bed falling onto your stomach, keeping your body tight and slightly dished. Ask your parents first!

Conditioning exercises

1. Practise dishing on your stomach and your back (see page 56).
2. Practise holding press-ups with either your hands or your feet raised from the ground level.
3. Practise rolling yourself backwards into a handstand and then moving over onto your feet. Keep your legs straight throughout.

Practice exercises 1 and 2.

Vaulting

This move is common to both ladies' and men's work and a lot of situations can be set up at home to help develop the work on this piece of apparatus. The vault consists of the following parts:

1. The run-up: the men have a maximum length of run-up of 25 metres, while the ladies can choose whatever distance they wish. The run-up is not judged.
2. The take-off: should be mechanically sound to provide elevation of the gymnast. It is not judged.
3. The flight-on: must be fast and the legs should be together.
4. The flight-off: should be of sufficient height and length from the horse.
5. The shape: this gives the character of the vault.
6. The landing: should be shown in good form.
7. The direction: must be in line with the path of the run-up.

The run-up

The run-up should be a sprinting action where the body is leaning slightly forwards. The head should be held naturally, with the eyes focussed on the horse and the springboard. The arms should swing to the sides of the body and be kept in line so that they do not cross in front of the body. The angle at the elbows should be approximately 90 degrees with the hands just reaching the height of the shoulders. The legs should have a short stride moving rapidly over their stride length. The objective is to hit the board at full speed while retaining energy to thrust off the horse. The length of the run-up will depend on the age and aerobic fitness of the gymnast.

The vault.

Practice exercises

1. Practise the running action while facing a mirror. Check your arms are by your sides.
2. Practise short runs, checking your leg and arm actions.
3. Put a large object in front of yourself which will stop your arms crossing in front of you. You can ask a friend to run with this in place too.
4. Ask a friend to tie a scarf or rope about your waist. Holding onto this he/she can run with you while holding you back slightly. This will make you lean forward into the correct running position.

Conditioning exercises

1. Practise general running and sprinting activities.

Practice exercise 3.

GYMNASTICS

The take-off

The arms start to move backwards as the legs come together in a hop to land with both feet on the board. During the hop the arms start to swing forwards while the legs move forwards to press down onto the board. On contact with the board, the legs should be in front of the body and behind the feet. The arms continue to swing forwards and upwards as the legs straighten off the board. The action off the board should be fast enabling the body to get into a straight position as soon as possible. This action sets up a rotation in the body ready for the flight-on.

Practice exercises

1. Take off from one foot with arms up and ahead and jump to two feet together. Use a hoop or line to mark the landing.
2. Repeat practice 1, but swing the arms down and back as you make the landing.
3. Add a run-up before the jump.
4. Jump up and out of the hoop, arms up and ahead.
5. Add a run-up before jumping out of the hoop.

Conditioning exercises

Squat jumps and ankle elevations as described on page 44.

The flight-on

The body should be stretched and slightly dished. The head is kept in natural line with the eyes fixed on the horse. The hands should reach forward to take contact first.

Practice exercises

Not really suitable unless you have a swimming pool!

Conditioning exercises

1. Rest feet on the wall in the position shown, first dish the body and tighten it. Slowly relax the body and let the chest sag down.

Again dish and tighten the body to experience the correct shape needed.
2. Lie on your stomach on a raised surface and raise your feet up as high as possible.
3. Practise jumping-press-ups.

The flight-off

This is difficult to practise at home except for the shape of the body. In flight-off, the body should rise so that the hip is at least a metre above the horse and the landing should be about 2 metres from the horse. The path described follows a parabolic curve.

The shape

This will be determined by the type of vault you are performing. Each one is in a structure group which the FIG lists in the *Code of Points*.

The landing

The legs should contact the floor in front of the line of the body. As the landing takes place, the legs should bend into a demi-plié while the arms are kept up and slightly behind the head. As the movement is absorbed by the legs, the arms move sideways down, to finish standing upright.

Practice exercises

1. Jump and land
2. Increase the height.

Conditioning exercise

Squat jumps into a demi-plié position.

Practice exercises 1 and 2.

USEFUL
ADDRESSES

British Amateur Gymnastics Association (BAGA)
Technical Department
Ford Hall
Lilleshall National Sports Centre
Nr. Newport
Shropshire
TF10 9NB

British Amateur Gymnastics Association (BAGA)
Publications Department
The Ghyll Industrial Estate
Heathfield
East Sussex
TW21 3AW

Association of British Gymnastic Coaches
The Secretary
Sherwood House
Hinckley Road
Burbage
Leicestershire
LE10 2AG

The Gymnast Magazine
World Wide Subscriptions Service Ltd
Unit 4
Gibbs Reed Farm
Pashley Road
Ticehurst
Wadhurst
East Sussex
TN5 7HE

Grasp Magazine
The Editor
Main Street
Bruntingthorpe
Leicestershire
LE17 5QF

National Coaching Foundation
4 College Close
Beckett Park
Leeds
LS6 3QH

National Sports Councils
For the Regional Office nearest to you
telephone the relevant country:
England: 071–388 1277
Scotland: 031–225 8411
N. Ireland: 0232–661222
Wales: 0222–397571

Most worldwide Organisations can be found via:
The International Gymnastic Federation (The FIG)
Rue des Oeuches 10
Case Postale 333
2740 Moutier 1
Suisse

INDEX

Figures in **bold** *refer to photographs.*